Celebrate R

# Getting Right with God, Yourself, and Others

## *The Journey Begins*

PARTICIPANT'S GUIDE 3

**John Baker** is the founder of Celebrate Recovery®, a ministry started at Saddleback Church. It is estimated that over the last 25 years more than 1.5 million people have gone through this Christ-centered recovery program. There are currently over 27,000 churches that have weekly Celebrate Recovery meetings.

John has been on staff since Celebrate Recovery started. He has served as the Pastor of Membership, the Pastor of Ministries, and is currently the Pastor of Saddleback Church's Signature Ministries. He is also serving as one of the nine Elder Pastors at Saddleback. John is a nationally known speaker and trainer in helping churches start Celebrate Recovery ministries.

John's writing accomplishments include Celebrate Recovery's *The Journey Begins* Curriculum, *Life's Healing Choices*, the *Celebrate Recovery Study Bible* (general editor), and *The Landing* and *Celebration Place* (coauthor). John's newest books are *Your First Step to Celebrate Recovery* and *The Celebrate Recovery Devotional* (coauthor).

John and his wife Cheryl, the cofounder of Celebrate Recovery, have been married for more than four decades and have served together in Celebrate Recovery since the beginning. They have two adult children, Laura and Johnny, and five grandchildren.

---

**Johnny Baker** has been on staff at Celebrate Recovery since 2004 and has been the Pastor of Celebrate Recovery at Saddleback Church since 2012. As an adult child of an alcoholic who chose to become an alcoholic himself, Johnny is passionate about breaking the cycle of dysfunction in his family and helping other families find the tools that will lead to healing and openness. He knows that because of Jesus Christ, and by continuing to stay active in Celebrate Recovery, Maggie, Chloe, and Jimmy—his three children—will never see him drink. Johnny is a nationally recognized speaker, trainer, and teacher of Celebrate Recovery. He is a coauthor of the *Celebrate Recovery Daily Devotional*, *Celebration Place*, and *The Landing*, and is an associate editor of the *Celebrate Recovery Study Bible*. He has been married since 2000 to his wife Jeni, who serves alongside him in Celebrate Recovery.

REVISED EDITION

# Celebrate Recovery®

# Getting Right with God, Yourself, and Others

## Participant's Guide 3

## *The Journey Begins*

A recovery program based on
eight principles from the Beatitudes

John Baker

Foreword by Rick Warren

ZONDERVAN®

ZONDERVAN

*Getting Right with God, Yourself, and Others*


Requests for information should be addressed to:
Zondervan, 3900 *Sparks Drive SE, Grand Rapids, Michigan 49546*

ISBN 978-0-310-13142-7 (softcover)
ISBN 978-0-310-13143-4 (ebook)



*Interior design: Michelle Espinoza*

*Printed in the United States of America*

# Contents

# Foreword by Rick Warren

You've undoubtedly heard the expression "Time heals all wounds." Unfortunately, it isn't true. As a pastor I frequently talk with people who are still carrying hurts from thirty or forty years ago. The truth is, time often makes things worse. Wounds that are left untended fester and spread infection throughout your entire body. Time only extends the pain if the problem isn't dealt with.

Celebrate Recovery® is a biblical and balanced program that can help you overcome your hurts, habits, and hang-ups. Based on the actual words of Jesus rather than psychological theory, this recovery program is more effective in helping people change than anything else I've seen or heard of. Over the years I've witnessed how the Holy Spirit has used this program to transform literally thousands of lives at Saddleback Church and help people grow toward full Christlike maturity.

Perhaps you are familiar with the classic 12-Step program of AA and other groups. While undoubtedly many lives have been helped through the 12 Steps, I've always been uncomfortable with that program's vagueness about the nature of God, the saving power of Jesus Christ, and the ministry of the Holy Spirit. So I began an intense study of the Scriptures to discover what God had to say about "recovery." To my amazement, I found the principles of recovery — in their logical order — given by Christ in His most famous message, the Sermon on the Mount.

My study resulted in a ten-week series of messages called "The Road to Recovery." During that series my associate pastor John Baker developed the four participant's guides, which became the heart of our Celebrate Recovery program.

As you work through these participant's guides, I trust that you will come to realize many benefits from this program. Most of all, however, my prayer for you is that, through Celebrate Recovery, you will find deep peace and lasting freedom in Jesus Christ as you walk your own road to recovery.

Dr. Rick Warren
Senior Pastor, Saddleback Church

# Introduction

Congratulations! You are well on your way on your road to recovery. You began by "Stepping Out of Denial into God's Grace." Next you made the major commitment to your continued growth in recovery by completing your spiritual inventory. That took a lot of effort and courage, but you will see some of the rewards of all your hard work as you finish Principle 4. The truth found in James 5:16 will take on new meaning in your life: "Confess your sins to each other and pray for each other so that you may be *healed*" (italics added).

After you CONFESS your sins, you will receive God's complete and perfect forgiveness. When you ADMIT your wrongs and share your inventory with another, you will experience further healing. As you become entirely READY to work through Principle 5, you will experience God's VICTORY in removing your defects of character that may have plagued you all your life.

Principle 6 will show you how to make your AMENDS and offer FORGIVENESS, so that you can be a model of God's GRACE as you get right with others.

In His steps,
John Baker

# The Road to Recovery

## Eight Principles Based on the Beatitudes

By Pastor Rick Warren

1. **R**ealize I'm not God. I admit that I am powerless to control my tendency to do the wrong thing and that my life is unmanageable.
   *"Happy are those who know they are spiritually poor."*
   *(Matthew 5:3)*
2. **E**arnestly believe that God exists, that I matter to Him, and that He has the power to help me recover.
   *"Happy are those who mourn, for they shall be comforted."*
   *(Matthew 5:4)*
3. **C**onsciously choose to commit all my life and will to Christ's care and control.
   *"Happy are the meek." (Matthew 5:5)*
4. **O**penly examine and confess my faults to myself, to God, and to someone I trust.
   *"Happy are the pure in heart." (Matthew 5:8)*
5. **V**oluntarily submit to every change God wants to make in my life and humbly ask Him to remove my character defects.
   *"Happy are those whose greatest desire is to do what God requires."*
   *(Matthew 5:6)*
6. **E**valuate all my relationships. Offer forgiveness to those who have hurt me and make amends for harm I've done to others, except when to do so would harm them or others.
   *"Happy are the merciful." (Matthew 5:7)*
   *"Happy are the peacemakers." (Matthew 5:9)*
7. **R**eserve a daily time with God for self-examination, Bible reading, and prayer in order to know God and His will for my life and to gain the power to follow His will.
8. **Y**ield myself to God to be used to bring this Good News to others, both by my example and by my words.
   *"Happy are those who are persecuted because they do what God requires." (Matthew 5:10)*

# Twelve Steps and Their Biblical Comparisons*

1. We admitted we were powerless over our addictions and compulsive behaviors, that our lives had become unmanageable.

   *"For I know that good itself does not dwell in me, that is, in my sinful nature. For I have the desire to do what is good, but I cannot carry it out." (Romans 7:18)*

2. We came to believe that a power greater than ourselves could restore us to sanity.

   *"For it is God who works in you to will and to act in order to fulfill his good purpose." (Philippians 2:13)*

3. We made a decision to turn our lives and our wills over to the care of God.

   *"Therefore, I urge you, brothers and sisters, in view of God's mercy, to offer your bodies as a living sacrifice, holy and pleasing to God — this is your true and proper worship." (Romans 12:1)*

4. We made a searching and fearless moral inventory of ourselves.

   *"Let us examine our ways and test them, and let us return to the Lord." (Lamentations 3:40)*

5. We admitted to God, to ourselves, and to another human being the exact nature of our wrongs.

   *"Therefore confess your sins to each other and pray for each other so that you may be healed." (James 5:16)*

6. We were entirely ready to have God remove all these defects of character.

   *"Humble yourselves before the Lord, and he will lift you up." (James 4:10)*

7. We humbly asked Him to remove all our shortcomings.

*"If we confess our sins, he is faithful and just and will forgive us our sins and purify us from all unrighteousness." (1 John 1:9)*

8. We made a list of all persons we had harmed and became willing to make amends to them all.

*"Do to others as you would have them do to you." (Luke 6:31)*

9. We made direct amends to such people whenever possible, except when to do so would injure them or others.

*"Therefore, if you are offering your gift at the altar and there remember that your brother or sister has something against you, leave your gift there in front of the altar. First go and be reconciled to them; then come and offer your gift." (Matthew 5:23 – 24)*

10. We continued to take personal inventory and when we were wrong, promptly admitted it.

*"So, if you think you are standing firm, be careful that you don't fall!" (1 Corinthians 10:12)*

11. We sought through prayer and meditation to improve our conscious contact with God, praying only for knowledge of His will for us and power to carry that out.

*"Let the message of Christ dwell among you richly." (Colossians 3:16)*

12. Having had a spiritual experience as the result of these steps, we try to carry this message to others and to practice these principles in all our affairs.

*"Brothers and sisters, if someone is caught in a sin, you who live by the Spirit should restore that person gently. But watch yourselves, or you also may be tempted." (Galatians 6:1)*

* Throughout this material, you will notice several references to the Christ-centered 12 Steps. Our prayer is that Celebrate Recovery will create a bridge to the millions of people who are familiar with the secular 12 Steps (I acknowledge the use of some material from the 12 Suggested Steps of Alcoholics Anonymous) and in so doing, introduce them to the one and only true Higher Power, Jesus Christ. Once they begin that relationship, asking Christ into their hearts as Lord and Savior, true healing and recovery can begin!

# Serenity Prayer

If you have attended secular recovery programs, you have seen the first four lines of the "Prayer for Serenity." The following is the complete prayer. I encourage you to pray it daily as you work through the principles!

**Prayer for Serenity**

*God, grant me the serenity*
*to accept the things I cannot change,*
*the courage to change the things I can,*
*and the wisdom to know the difference.*
*Living one day at a time,*
*enjoying one moment at a time ;*
*accepting hardship as a pathway to peace ;*
*taking, as Jesus did,*
*this sinful world as it is,*
*not as I would have it ;*
*trusting that You will make all things right*
*if I surrender to Your will ;*
*so that I may be reasonably happy in this life*
*and supremely happy with You forever in the next.*
*Amen.*

Reinhold Niebuhr

# Celebrate Recovery's Small Group Guidelines

The following five guidelines will ensure that your small group is a safe place. They need to be read at the beginning of every meeting.

1. Keep your sharing focused on your own thoughts and feelings. Limit your sharing to three to five minutes.
2. There is NO cross talk. Cross talk is when two individuals engage in conversation excluding all others. Each person is free to express his or her feelings without interruptions.
3. We are here to support one another, not "fix" another.
4. Anonymity and confidentiality are basic requirements. What is shared in the group stays in the group. The only exception is when someone threatens to injure themselves or others.
5. Offensive language has no place in a Christ-centered recovery group.

Lesson 12

# Confess

**Principle 4**: Openly examine and confess my faults to myself, to God, and to someone I trust.

*"Happy are the pure in heart." (Matthew 5:8)*

**Step 5**: We admitted to God, to ourselves, and to another human being the exact nature of our wrongs.

*"Therefore confess your sins to each other and pray for each other so that you may be healed." (James 5:16)*

## Think About It

After writing an inventory, we must deal with what we have written. The first way we do that is to confess our sins to God. Let's review the acrostic for CONFESS.

**C**onfess your shortcomings, resentments, and sins

God wants us to come clean. We need to admit that "what is wrong is wrong. We're guilty as charged." We need to own up to the sins we discovered in our inventory.

*"Whoever conceals their sins does not prosper, but the one who confesses and renounces them finds mercy." (Proverbs 28:13)*

**O**bey God's directions

Principle 4 sums up God's directions for confessing our sins.

1. We confess our sins to God.

*" 'As surely as I am the living God, says the Lord, everyone will kneel before me, and everyone will confess that I am God.' Every one of us, then, will have to give an account to God." (Romans 14:11 – 12, GNT)*

2. We share them with another person whom we trust:

*"Therefore confess your sins to each other and pray for each other so that you may be healed." (James 5:16)*

**N**o more guilt

This step begins to restore our confidence and our relationships and allows us to move on from our "rearview mirror" living. In Romans 8:1 we are assured that "there is now no condemnation for those who are in Christ Jesus."

*"All of have sinned; . . . yet now God declares us 'not guilty' . . . if we trust in Jesus Christ, who . . . freely takes away our sins." (Romans 3:23 – 24, TLB)*

The "CON" is over! We have followed God's directions on how to confess our wrongs. Four very positive things start to happen after we "FESS" up.

**F**ace the truth

Recovery requires honesty! After we complete this principle we can allow the light of God's truth to heal our hurts, hang-ups, and habits. We stop denying our true feelings.

*"Jesus . . . said, 'I am the light of the world. Whoever follows me will never walk in darkness, but will have the light of life.'" (John 8:12)*

*"Then you will know the truth, and the truth will set you free."*
*(John 8:32)*

## Ease the pain

"We are only as sick as our secrets!" When we share our deepest secrets we divide the pain and the shame. We begin to see a healthy self-worth develop, one that is no longer based on the world's standards, but on those of Jesus Christ.

*"There was a time when I wouldn't admit what a sinner I was. But my dishonesty made me miserable and filled my days with frustration. . . . My strength evaporated like water on a sunny day until I finally admitted all my sins to you and stopped trying to hide them. I said to myself, 'I will confess them to the Lord.' And you forgave me! All my guilt is gone." (Psalm 32:3 – 5, TLB)*

## Stop the blame

We cannot find peace and serenity if we continue to blame ourselves or others. Our secrets have isolated us from each other. They have prevented intimacy in all our relationships.

*"Why do you look at the speck of sawdust in your brother's eye and fail to notice the plank in your own? How can you say to your brother, 'Let me get the speck out of your eye,' when there is a plank in your own? . . . Take the plank out of your own eye first, and then you can see clearly enough to remove your brother's speck of dust." (Matthew 7:3, PH)*

## Start accepting God's forgiveness

Once we accept God's forgiveness we can look others in the eye. We understand ourselves and our past actions in a "new light." We are ready to find the humility to exchange our shortcomings in Principle 5.

*"For God was in Christ, restoring the world to himself, no longer counting men's sins against them but blotting them out."*
*(2 Corinthians 5:19, TLB)*

*"But if we confess our sins, he will forgive our sins, because we can trust God to do what is right. He will cleanse us from all the wrongs we have done." (1 John 1:9, NCV)*

**Write About It**

1. What wrongs, resentments, or secret sins are keeping you awake at night? Wouldn't you like to get rid of them?

2. What value do you see in confessing, in coming clean of the wreckage of your past?

3. As you obey God's directions for confession, what results do you expect God to produce in your life?

4. What freedom do you feel because of the words of Romans 8:1 and Romans 3:23 – 24? What specifically do the phrases "no condemnation" and "not guilty" mean to you?

5. After you complete Principle 4, you will find four areas of your life begin to improve. You will be able to face the truth, ease the pain, stop the blame, and start accepting God's forgiveness. In what areas of your life will each of these four positive changes help your recovery?

   I can be more honest with. . .

   I can ease my pain by. . .

I can stop blaming. . .

I can accept God's forgiveness because of. . .

Lesson 13

# ADMIT

**Principle 4**: Openly examine and confess my faults to myself, to God, and to someone I trust.

*"Happy are the pure in heart." (Matthew 5:8)*

**Step 5**: We admitted to God, to ourselves, and to another human being the exact nature of our wrongs.

*"Therefore confess your sins to each other and pray for each other so that you may be healed." (James 5:16)*

## Think About It

People often ask me why they need to admit their wrongs to another person. There are three main reasons.

### Why admit my wrongs?

1. *We gain healing that the Bible promises.*

Look at James 5:16 again. God's Word tells us that we are to admit our wrongs, our sins, to *one another.* You do this not to receive their forgiveness, for God already forgave you when you confessed your wrongs and sins to Him. James 5:16 says to confess your sins to one another for *healing*.

Sharing our secrets, struggles, and failures with another is part of God's plan of our healing process. The road to recovery is not meant to be walked alone.

2. *We gain freedom.*

Our secrets have kept us in chains, bound up, frozen, and unable to move in all our relationships. Admitting our sins *snaps* the chains.

> *"They cried to the Lord in their troubles, and he rescued them! He led them from the darkness and the shadow of death and snapped their chains." (Psalm 107:13 – 14, TLB)*

3. *We gain support.*

When you share your inventory with another person, you get support. The person can keep you focused and provide feedback. He or she can challenge you when denial surfaces. Most important, the person will listen!

**How do I choose someone?**

1. Choose someone of the same sex as you whom you trust and respect.
2. Ask your sponsor or accountability partner. Just be sure they have completed Principle 4 (or Steps 4 and 5).
3. Set up an appointment with the person, a time without interruptions! It usually takes two to three hours to share your inventory.

**Guidelines for your meeting**

1. Start with prayer. Ask for courage, humility, and honesty. Here is a sample prayer:

   *God, I ask that You fill me with Your peace and strength during my sharing of my inventory. I know that You have forgiven me for my past wrongs, my sins. Thank You for sending Your Son to pay the price for me, so my sins can be forgiven. During this meeting help me to be humble and completely honest. Thank You for providing me with this program and ________________ (the name of the person with whom you are sharing your inventory). Thank You for allowing the chains of my past to be snapped. In my Savior's name I pray, Amen.*

2. Read the Principle 4 verses found on pages 25 and 26 in this participant's guide.
3. Keep your sharing balanced — weaknesses and strengths!
4. End in prayer. Thank God for the tools He has given to you and for the complete forgiveness found in Christ!

*"But if we confess our sins, he will forgive our sins, because we can trust God to do what is right. He will cleanse us from all the wrongs we have done." (1 John 1:9, NCV)*

## Write About It

1. In Principle 4 we are asked to give our inventory three times. Who are we to confess it to and why?

2. Most of us find it easier to confess our wrongs to ourselves and God. We seem to have more difficulty in sharing them with another person. What is the most difficult part for you? Why?

3. What is your biggest fear of sharing your inventory with another person?

4. List three people with whom you are considering sharing your inventory. List the pros and cons of each selection. Circle your final choice.

5. Pick a quiet location to share your inventory. List three places and circle the best one.

Now you are ready for one of the most freeing experiences of your life here on this earth! You will appreciate James 5:16 as never before. "Therefore confess your sins to each other and pray for each other so that you may be healed."

# Principle 4 Verses

*"Admit your faults to one another and pray for each other so that you may be healed." (James 5:16, TLB)*

*"You were dead in sins, and your sinful desires were not yet cut away. Then he gave you a share in the very life of Christ, for he forgave all your sins, and blotted out the charges proved against you, the list of his commandments which you had not obeyed. He took this list of sins and destroyed it by nailing it to Christ's cross. In this way God took away Satan's power to accuse you of sin, and God openly displayed to the whole world Christ's triumph at the cross where your sins were all taken away."*
*(Colossians 2:13 – 15, TLB)*

*"If we say that we have no sin, we are only fooling ourselves, and refusing to accept the truth. But if we confess our sins to him, he can be depended on to forgive us and to cleanse us from every wrong. (And it is perfectly proper for God to do this for us because Christ died to wash away our sins.)"*
*(1 John 1:8 – 9, TLB)*

*"For God was in Christ, restoring the world to himself, no longer counting men's sins against them but blotting them out. This is the wonderful message he has given us to tell others."*
*(2 Corinthians 5:19, TLB)*

*"A man who refuses to admit his mistakes can never be successful. But if he confesses and forsakes them, he gets another chance."*
*(Proverbs 28:13, TLB)*

*"Yes, each of us will give an account of himself to God."*
*(Romans 14:12, TLB)*

*"There was a time when I wouldn't admit what a sinner I was. But my dishonesty made me miserable and filled my days with frustration. All day and all night your hand was heavy on me. My strength evaporated like water on a sunny day until I finally admitted all my sins to you and stopped trying to hide them. I said to myself, 'I will confess them to the Lord.' And you forgave me! All my guilt is gone." (Psalm 32:3 – 5, TLB)*

*"So there is now no condemnation awaiting those who belong to Christ Jesus." (Romans 8:1, TLB)*

# READY

**Principle 5**: Voluntarily submit to every change God wants to make in my life and humbly ask Him to remove my character defects.

*"Happy are those whose greatest desire is to do what God requires."*
*(Matthew 5:6)*

**Step 6**: We were entirely ready to have God remove all these defects of character.

*"Humble yourselves before the Lord, and he will lift you up."*
*(James 4:10)*

## Think About It

What does it mean to be entirely READY to have God remove our character defects?

**R**elease control

God is a gentleman. In Principle 3 He didn't force His will on you. He waited for you to invite Him in! Now in Principle 5 you need to be entirely ready, willing to let God into every area of your life. He won't come in where He is not welcomed.

It has been said that "willingness is the key that goes into the lock and opens the door that allows God to begin to remove your character defects."

*"Help me to do your will, for you are my God. Lead me in good paths, for your Spirit is good." (Psalm 143:10, TLB)*

**E**asy does it

These principles and steps are not quick fixes! You need to allow time for God to work in your life. This principle goes further than helping you to stop doing wrong. It goes after the very defect that causes you to sin! *It takes time!*

*"Commit everything you do to the Lord. Trust him to help you do it and he will." (Psalm 37:5, TLB)*

**A**ccept the change

Seeing the need for change and allowing the change to occur are two different things. Principle 5 will not work if you are still trapped by your self-will. You need to be ready to accept God's help throughout the transition.

*"So then, have your minds ready for action. Keep alert and set your hope completely on the blessing which will be given you when Jesus Christ is revealed. Be obedient to God, and do not allow your lives to be shaped by those desires you had when you were still ignorant." (1 Peter 1:13 – 14, GNT)*

**D**o replace your character defects

You spent a lot of time with your old hang-ups, compulsions, obsessions, and habits. When God removes one, you need to replace it with something positive, such as recovery meetings, church, service, and volunteering! If you don't, you open yourself for a negative character defect to return.

*"When an evil spirit goes out of a person it travels over dry country looking for a place to rest. If it can't find one, it says to itself, 'I will go back to my house.' So it goes back and finds the house empty, . . . . Then it goes out and brings along seven other spirits even worse than itself, and they come and live there." (Matthew 12:43 – 45, GNT)*

## Yield to the growth

Your old self-doubts and low self-esteem may tell you that you are not worthy of the growth and progress that you are making in the program. Yield to the growth — it is the Holy Spirit's work within you.

*"The person who has been born into God's family does not make a practice of sinning, because now God's life is in him; so he can't keep on sinning, for this new life has been born into him and controls him — he has been born again." (1 John 3:9, TLB)*

Are you entirely ready — willing — to voluntarily submit to any and all changes God wants to make in your life? If you are, read the Principle 5a verses on page 32 and pray the following prayer:

*Dear God, thank You for taking me this far in my recovery journey. Now I pray for Your help in making me be entirely ready to change all my shortcomings. Give me the strength to deal with all of my character defects that I have turned over to You. Allow me to accept all the changes that You want to make in me. Help me be the person that You want me to be. In Your Son's name I pray, Amen.*

---

**Write About It**

1. Have you released control? (If not, review Principle 3: "Consciously choose to commit all my life and will to Christ's care and control.")

    - List the areas of your life that you have been able to turn over and surrender to Jesus Christ.

- List the areas of your life that you are still holding on to, attempting to control them on your own power.

2. What does the phrase "easy does it" mean to you? What area of your recovery are you attempting to rush — looking for the "quick fix"?

3. Explain the differences in seeing a need for change and being entirely ready to accept positive change in your recovery.

4. It is very important that you allow God to replace your character defects with positive changes. What are some of the positive changes that you could make in your recovery? In your family? In your job?

5. Sometimes it is difficult for us in recovery to see the positive changes that God is making in our lives. Have you been able to accept and enjoy your growth? How?

# Principle 5a Verses

*"Humble yourselves before the Lord, and he will lift you up."*
*(James 4:10)*

*"So get rid of all that is wrong in your life, both inside and outside, and humbly be glad for the wonderful message we have received, for it is able to save our souls as it takes hold of our hearts."*
*(James 1:21, TLB)*

*"For I can never forget these awful years; always my soul will live in utter shame. Yet there is one ray of hope: his compassion never ends. It is only the Lord's mercies that have kept us from complete destruction." (Lamentations 3:20 – 22, TLB)*

*"O loving and kind God, have mercy. Have pity upon me and take away the awful stain of my transgressions. Oh, wash me, cleanse me from this guilt. Let me be pure again."*
*(Psalm 51:1 – 2, TLB)*

Lesson 15

# VICTORY

**Principle 5**: Voluntarily submit to every change God wants to make in my life and humbly ask Him to remove my character defects.

*"Happy are those whose greatest desire is to do what God requires." (Matthew 5:6)*

**Step 6**: We were entirely ready to have God remove all these defects of character.

*"Humble yourselves before the Lord, and he will lift you up." (James 4:10)*

**Step 7**: We humbly asked Him to remove all our shortcomings.

*"If we confess our sins, he is faithful and just and will forgive us our sins and purify us from all unrighteousness." (1 John 1:9)*

## Think About It

How can you have VICTORY over your defects of character?

**V**oluntarily submit

Voluntarily submit to every change God wants me to make in my life and humbly ask Him to remove my shortcomings.

*"Offer yourselves as a living sacrifice to God, dedicated to his service and pleasing to him. . . . Let God transform you inwardly by a complete change of your mind." (Romans 12:1 – 2, GNT)*

In Principle 3 we made a decision to turn our lives over to God's will. Now "you are entirely ready to have God remove all your defects of character" (Step 6).

It is important to understand that Principle 5 is a process. Lasting change takes time. The remainder of this lesson outlines the process to have God make the positive changes in your life that you and He both desire.

## Identify character defects

Identify which character defects you want to work on first. Go back to the wrongs, shortcomings, and sins you discovered in your inventory. Ask God to first remove those that are causing the most pain.

*"In their hearts humans plan their course, but the LORD establishes their steps." (Proverbs 16:9)*

## Change your mind

When you become a Christian you are a new creation — a brand new person inside; the old nature is gone. But you have to let God (change) transform you by renewing your mind. The changes that are going to take place are a result of a team effort — your responsibility is to take the action to follow God's directions for change.

*"Do not conform to the pattern of this world, but be transformed by the renewing of your mind. Then you will be able to test and approve what God's will is — his good, pleasing and perfect will." (Romans 12:2)*

## Turn over character defects

Turn your character defects over to Jesus Christ. Relying on your own willpower has blocked your recovery. You have tried to change your hurts, hang-ups, and habits by yourself and were unsuccessful. "Let go; let God."

*"Humble yourselves before the Lord, and he will lift you up."*
*(James 4:10)*

*"The Lord is faithful, and he will strengthen you and protect you from the evil one." (2 Thessalonians 3:3)*

## **O**ne day at a time

Recovery works one day at a time! Your lifelong hurts, hang-ups, and habits need to be worked on in twenty-four-hour increments. "Life by the yard is hard; life by the inch is a cinch."

*"So don't be anxious about tomorrow. God will take care of your tomorrow too. Live one day at a time." (Matthew 6:34, TLB)*

## **R**ecovery is a process

Once you ask God to remove your character defects, you begin a journey that will lead you to new freedom from your past. Don't look for perfection; instead rejoice in steady progress.

*"And I am sure that God who began a good work within you will keep right on helping you grow in his grace until his task within you is finally finished on that day when Jesus Christ returns."*
*(Philippians 1:6, TLB)*

## **Y**ou must choose to change

To ask for help to change your hurts, hang-ups, and habits requires humility. We need to stop trying to make the changes on our power. We need to "humbly ask Him to remove all our shortcomings." We need to rely on His power to change us!

*"God gives strength to the humble, . . . so give yourselves humbly to God. Resist the devil and he will flee from you. And when you draw close to God, God will draw close to you." (James 4:6 – 8, TLB)*

## Principle 5 Prayer

*Dear God, show me Your will in working on my shortcomings. Help me not to resist the changes that You have planned for me. I need You to "direct my steps." Help me stay in today, not get dragged back into the past or lost in the future. I ask You to give me the power and the wisdom to make the very best I can out of today. In Christ's name I pray, Amen.*

---

### Write About It

1. As you *voluntarily* submit to every change God wants you to make in your recovery, how does Romans 12:1 – 2 help you know that real, positive change is possible?

2. In Principle 5 you need to ask God to help you identify the defects of character that you need to work on first. List the changes that you want to ask God to help you work on now. Will you work on them?

3. God's Word teaches us that real change comes from the changing of our minds. We must take the positive action required to follow God's directions. List the actions that you need to take to begin working on the defects of character that you listed in question 2.

   ACTION PLAN

   (Read the Principle 5b Verses on page 39.)

   Defect of character:

   I need to stop doing:

   I need to start doing:

4. List the specific ways that you have turned from relying on your own willpower to relying on God's will for your life.

5. What does the phrase "one day at a time" mean to you and your recovery?

6. It has been stated that "Recovery is not perfection; it is a process." Do you agree with that? Why?

7. What does humility mean to you? How will being humble allow you to change?

# Principle 5b Verses

*"If we confess our sins, he is faithful and just and will forgive us our sins and purify us from all unrighteousness." (1 John 1:9)*

*"Don't copy the behavior and customs of this world, but be a new and different person with a fresh newness in all you do and think. Then you will learn from your own experience how his ways will really satisfy you." (Romans 12:2, TLB)*

*"If you want to know what God wants you to do, ask him, and he will gladly tell you, for he is always ready to give a bountiful supply of wisdom to all who ask him; he will not resent it." (James 1:5, TLB)*

*"But he gives us more and more strength to stand against all such evil longings. As the Scripture says, God gives strength to the humble, but sets himself against the proud and haughty. So give yourselves humbly to God. Resist the devil and he will flee from you." (James 4:6 – 7, TLB)*

*"And when you draw close to God, God will draw close to you. Wash your hands, you sinners, and let your hearts be filled with God alone to make them pure and true to him." (James 4:8, TLB)*

*"Humble yourselves before the Lord, and he will lift you up." (James 4:10)*

*"Now glory be to God who by his mighty power at work within us is able to do far more than we would ever dare to ask or even dream of — infinitely beyond our highest prayers, desires, thoughts, or hopes." (Ephesians 3:20, TLB)*

# AMENDS

**Principle 6**: Evaluate all my relationships. Offer forgiveness to those who have hurt me and make amends for harm I've done to others, except when to do so would harm them or others.

*"Happy are the merciful." (Matthew 5:7)*
*"Happy are the peacemakers." (Matthew 5:9)*

**Step 8**: We made a list of all persons we had harmed and became willing to make amends to them all.

*"Do to others as you would have them do to you." (Luke 6:31)*

## Think About It

Making your amends is the beginning of the end of your isolation from others and God. The AMENDS acrostic will help you get started.

**A**dmit the hurt and the harm

You need to once again face the hurts, resentments, and wrongs others have caused you, or wrongs that you have caused others. Holding on to resentments not only blocks your recovery but blocks God's forgiveness in your life.

*"Do not judge others, and God will not judge you; do not condemn others, and God will not condemn you; forgive others, and God will forgive you." (Luke 6:37, GNT)*

## Make a list

Go back to your inventory sheets. In column 1 you will find the list of people who you need to forgive. In column 5 you will find the list of people to whom you owe amends. Are there any others you need to add?

*"Treat others as you want them to treat you." (Luke 6:31, TLB)*

## Encourage one another

Before you make your amends or offer your forgiveness to others you need to meet with your accountability partner or a sponsor. He or she will encourage you and give you a valuable objective opinion, which will ensure that your motives stay on track.

*"And let us consider how we may spur one another on toward love and good deeds." (Hebrews 10:24)*

## Not for them

You need to approach those to whom you are offering your forgiveness or amends humbly, sincerely, and willingly. Do not offer excuses or attempt to justify your actions. Focus only on your part. Don't expect anything back.

*"Love your enemies and do good to them, lend and expect nothing back." (Luke 6:35, GNT)*

## Do it at the right time

This step not only requires courage, good judgment, and willingness, but a careful sense of timing! It is *key* at this time to prayerfully ask Jesus Christ for His guidance and direction.

*"In humility value others above yourselves, not looking to your own interests but each of you to the interests of the others." (Philippians 2:3 – 4)*

## Start living the promises of recovery

As we complete this principle, we will discover God's gift of true freedom from our past. We will begin to find the peace and serenity that we have long been seeking. We will become ready to embrace God's purpose for our lives.

God promises, "I will repay you for the years the locusts have eaten" (Joel 2:25).

*"If it is possible, as far as it depends on you, live at peace with everyone." (Romans 12:18)*

### Principle 6a Prayer

*Dear God, I pray for willingness — willingness to evaluate all my past and current relationships. Please show me the people who I have hurt, and help me become willing to offer my amends to them. Also, God, give me Your strength to become willing to offer forgiveness to those who have hurt me. I pray for Your perfect timing for taking the action Principle 6 calls for. I ask all these things in Your Son's name, Amen.*

### Write About It

1. Once again you need to admit the past hurts — what others did to you and the harm that you caused to others. Explain how holding on to your past resentments and guilt has blocked your recovery. Be specific.

2. Next, you are ready to make your list. Use the following worksheet.

   List the names of those to whom you think you owe amends to in column 1. Then list those individuals who have hurt you and who you need to forgive in column 2. Keep this chart and see how God has increased your list within the next thirty days. Also, begin praying for the willingness and God's direction for you to complete this principle.

**Amends List**

| I OWE AMENDS TO . . . | I NEED TO FORGIVE . . . |
|---|---|

3. Who do you have on your recovery support team to encourage you as you make your amends and offer your forgiveness?

   SPONSOR:

   ACCOUNTABILITY PARTNERS:

4. What does the phrase "not for them" mean to you?

5. What does the phrase " don't expect anything back" mean to you?

6. Timing is so important in this step. List the individuals who could be possibly injured from your making an amends to them and why.

7. Go back to the "start living the promises" section of amends. List some of the promises of recovery that are coming true in your life!

Lesson 17

# FORGIVENESS

**Principle 6**: Evaluate all my relationships. Offer forgiveness to those who have hurt me and make amends for harm I've done to others, except when to do so would harm them or others.

*"Happy are the merciful." (Matthew 5:7)*
*"Happy are the peacemakers." (Matthew 5:9)*

**Step 8**: We made a list of all persons we had harmed and became willing to make amends to them all.

*"Do to others as you would have them do to you." (Luke 6:31)*

**Step 9**: We made direct amends to such people whenever possible, except when to do so would injure them or others.

*"Therefore, if you are offering your gift at the altar and there remember that your brother or sister has something against you, leave your gift there in front of the altar. First go and be reconciled to them; then come and offer your gift." (Matthew 5:23 – 24)*

## Think About It

Do you know the three kinds of forgiveness? To be completely free from your resentments, anger, fears, shame, and guilt, you need to give and accept forgiveness in all areas of your lives. If you do not, your recovery will be stalled and thus incomplete.

## Have you accepted God's forgiveness?

Have you really accepted Jesus' work on the cross? By His death on the cross all your sins were canceled — *paid in full!* He exclaimed from the cross, "It is finished" (John 19:30).

*"God puts people right through their faith in Jesus Christ. God does this to all who believe in Christ, because there is no difference at all: everyone has sinned and is far away from God's saving presence. But by the free gift of God's grace they are all put right with him through Christ Jesus, who sets them free. God offered him, so that by his blood he should become the means by which people's sins are forgiven through their faith in him." (Romans 3:22 – 25, GNT)*

## Have you forgiven others who have hurt you?

You must "let go" of the pain of the past harm and abuse caused by others. Until you are able to release it and forgive it, it will continue to hold you prisoner.

*"Do not repay anyone evil for evil. Be careful to do what is right in the eyes of everybody. If it is possible, as far as it depends on you, live at peace with everyone." (Romans 12:17 – 18)*

You may owe God an amends! Remember that the harm that others did to you was from their free will, not God's will.

*"After you have borne these sufferings a very little while, God himself (from whom we receive all grace and who has called you to share his eternal splendour through Christ) will make you whole and secure and strong." (1 Peter 5:10, PH)*

NOTE: If you have been the victim of sexual abuse, physical abuse, or childhood emotional abuse or neglect I am truly sorry for the pain you have suffered. I hurt with you. But you will not find the peace and freedom from your perpetrator until you are able to forgive that person. Remember, forgiving him or her in no way excuses the harm done against you. Forgiveness will allow you, however, to be released from the power that the person has had over you. I have rewritten Principle 6 (Steps 8 and 9) for you.

> Step 8: Make a list of all persons who have harmed us and become willing to seek God's help in forgiving our perpetrators, as well as forgiving ourselves. Realize we've also harmed others and become willing to make amends to them.
>
> Step 9: Extend forgiveness to ourselves and to others who have perpetrated against us, realizing this is an attitude of the heart, not always confrontation. Make direct amends, asking forgiveness from those people we have harmed, except when to do so would injure them or others.

## Have you forgiven yourself?

You may feel that the guilt and shame of your past is just too much to forgive. This is what God wants you to do with the darkness of your past: "Come, let's talk this over! says the Lord; no matter how deep the stain of your sins, I can take it out and make you as clean as freshly fallen snow. Even if you are stained as red as crimson, I can make you white as wool! If you will only let me help you" (Isaiah 1:18 – 19, TLB).

Remember, "Therefore, there is now no condemnation for those who are in Christ Jesus" (Romans 8:1).

---

**Write About It**

1. As you look at the three kinds of forgiveness, which one of them was the easiest for you to accept? Why?

2. Which area of forgiveness was the most difficult for you to accept? Why?

3. What do the words of Christ found in John 19:30 (“It is finished.”) mean to you?

4. What hurt(s) from a past relationship are you still holding on to?

5. How can you let go of the hurt(s)? Be specific.

6. Do you owe God an amends? When will you give it?

7. How have you been blaming God for the harmful actions that others took against you?

8. Have you forgiven yourself? What past actions in your life do you still feel guilt and shame about? (List them, pray about them, and work on them in the next lesson.)

# Principle 6a Verses

*"Treat others as you want them to treat you." (Luke 6:31, TLB)*

*"Be gentle and ready to forgive; never hold grudges. Remember, the Lord forgave you, so you must forgive others." (Colossians 3:13, TLB)*

*"You, therefore, have no excuse, you who pass judgment on someone else, for at whatever point you judge another, you are condemning yourself, because you who pass judgment do the same things." (Romans 2:1)*

*"Do not judge, and you will not be judged. Do not condemn, and you will not be condemned. Forgive, and you will be forgiven." (Luke 6:37)*

*". . . and forgive us our sins, just as we have forgiven those who have sinned against us." (Matthew 6:12, TLB)*

*"So what should we say about this? If God is with us, no one can defeat us." (Romans 8:31, NCV)*

Lesson 18

# GRACE

**Principle 6**: Evaluate all my relationships. Offer forgiveness to those who have hurt me and make amends for harm I've done to others, except when to do so would harm them or others.

*"Happy are the merciful." (Matthew 5:7)*
*"Happy are the peacemakers." (Matthew 5:9)*

**Step 9**: We made direct amends to such people whenever possible, except when to do so would injure them or others.

*"Therefore, if you are offering your gift at the altar and there remember that your brother or sister has something against you, leave your gift there in front of the altar. First go and be reconciled to them; then come and offer your gift." (Matthew 5:23 – 24)*

## Think About It

To complete Principle 6 we must make our amends, make restitution, offer our forgiveness, but most of all, we must receive and model Jesus Christ's freely given gift of GRACE.

*" 'My grace is enough for you. When you are weak, my power is made perfect in you.' So I am very happy to brag about my weaknesses. Then Christ's power can live in me. For this reason I am happy when I have weaknesses, insults, hard times, sufferings, and all kinds of troubles for Christ. Because when I am weak, then I am truly strong." (2 Corinthians 12:9 – 10, NCV)*

## **G**od's gift

Grace cannot be bought. It is a freely given gift by God to you and me. When we complete Principle 6, we are to offer (give) our amends and forgiveness and expect nothing back.

*"All need to be made right with God by his grace, which is a free gift. They need to be made free from sin through Jesus Christ." (Romans 3:24, NCV)*

*"Prepare your minds for service and have self-control. All your hope should be for the gift of grace that will be yours when Jesus Christ is shown to you." (1 Peter 1:13, NCV)*

## **R**eceived by our faith

We cannot work our way into heaven. Only by professing our faith in Christ as our Savior can we experience His grace and have eternal life. It is only through our faith in Christ that we can find the strength and courage needed for us to make our amends and offer our forgiveness.

*"For it is by grace you have been saved, through faith — and this is not from yourselves, it is the gift of God — not by works, so that no one can boast." (Ephesians 2:8 – 9)*

*"Through whom we have gained access by faith into this grace in which we now stand. And we boast in the hope of the glory of God." (Romans 5:2)*

## **A**ccepted by God's love

God loved us while we were still sinning. Grace is the love that gives, that loves the unlovely and the unlovable. We can love others because God first loved us, and we can also *forgive* others because God first forgave us.

*"Let us, then, feel very sure that we can come before God's throne where there is grace. There we can receive mercy and grace to help us when we need it." (Hebrews 4:16, NCV)*

*"Forgive us our debts, as we also have forgiven our debtors." (Matthew 6:12)*

*"If you forgive other people when they sin against you, your heavenly Father will also forgive you." (Matthew 6:14)*

## Christ paid the price

Jesus loves us so much that He died on the cross so that all our sins, all our wrongs, are forgiven. He paid the price and sacrificed Himself for us so that we may be with Him forever. We also need to sacrifice — our pride and our selfishness. We must speak the truth in love and focus on our part in making amends or offering forgiveness.

*"I do not set aside the grace of God, for if righteousness could be gained through the law, Christ died for nothing!" (Galatians 2:21)*

*"In Christ we are set free by the blood of his death, and so we have forgiveness of sins. How rich is God's grace." (Ephesians 1:7, NCV)*

## Everlasting gift

Once you have accepted Jesus Christ as your Lord and Savior, God's gift of grace is forever.

*"And I am sure that God who began the good work within you will keep right on helping you grow in his grace until his task within you is finally finished on that day when Jesus Christ returns." (Philippians 1:6, TLB)*

*"May our Lord Jesus Christ himself and God our Father encourage you and strengthen you in every good thing you do and say. God loved us, and through his grace he gave us a good hope and encouragement that continues forever." (2 Thessalonians 2:16, NCV)*

Now you are ready to start modeling God's grace by working Principle 6.

1. Take the names of the individuals that you listed on your "Amends List" (page 43).
2. Highlight the ones you can take care of immediately.
3. Review them one more time with your sponsor or accountability partner to ensure that making an amends or offering your forgiveness to the individual would not injure them or another.
4. Pray, asking God to show you the right time to make the amends or offer your forgiveness. Read the Principle 6b verses on page 57.
5. Develop a plan for making amends to those on your list that you cannot make immediately. If someone on your list has died or you cannot locate him or her, you can write the person a letter and share it with your support team.

## Principle 6b Prayer

*Dear God, thank You for Your love, for Your freely given grace. Help me model Your ways when I make my amends to those I have hurt and offer my forgiveness to those who have injured me. Help me to set aside my selfishness and speak the truth in love. I pray that I would focus only on my part, my responsibility in the issue. I know that I can forgive others because You first forgave me. Thank You for loving me. In Jesus' name I pray, Amen.*

**Write About It**

1. How has Jesus Christ used your weaknesses and turned them into strengths?

2. How can you receive God's gift of grace (Romans 5:2)?

3. How can you model God's gift of grace in making your amends?

4. In what ways have you experienced God's grace in your recovery?

5. God loved and accepted us while we were still sinners (Ephesians 2:5). How can you model that acceptance to those to whom you need to offer forgiveness or make amends?

6. In Principle 6 we are not trying to get even. Christ paid the price for all of our wrongs. What does "speaking the truth in love" mean to you?

7. Why is it important that you focus *only* on your part in making an amends or offering forgiveness?

8. List some of the things that God has shown you through working Principle 6.

# Principle 6b Verses

*"So if you are standing before the altar in the Temple, offering a sacrifice to God, and suddenly remember that a friend has something against you, leave your sacrifice there beside the altar and go and apologize and be reconciled to him, and then come and offer your sacrifice to God." (Matthew 5:23 – 24, TLB)*

*"If anyone says 'I love God,' but keeps on hating his brother, he is a liar; for if he doesn't love his brother who is right there in front of him, how can he love God whom he has never seen?" (1 John 4:20, TLB)*

*"Love your enemies! Do good to them! Lend to them! And don't be concerned about the fact that they won't repay. Then your reward from heaven will be very great, and you will truly be acting as sons of God: for he is kind to the unthankful and to those who are very wicked." (Luke 6:35, TLB)*

*"There is a saying, 'Love your friends and hate your enemies.' But I say: Love your enemies! Pray for those who persecute you!" (Matthew 5:43 – 44, TLB)*

*"Never pay back evil for evil. Do things in such a way that everyone can see you are honest clear through. Don't quarrel with anyone. Be at peace with everyone, just as much as possible." (Romans 12:17 – 18, TLB)*

*"Pay all your debts except the debt of love for others — never finish paying that! For if you love them, you will be obeying all of God's laws, fulfilling all his requirements." (Romans 13:8, TLB)*

# Afterword

When you have completed all seven lessons to the best of your ability, CONGRATULATIONS are most definitely in order! The freedom you found by working Principles 4 through 6 can only come from God and a lot of courageous effort from you. You have taken a giant step toward "getting right with God, yourself, and others!"

Remember that recovery is a journey, a process. God and you are going to be working on the changes in your life for many years to come, one day at a time!

Now you are ready for the last two principles of the program. Principles 7 and 8 are going to show you how to continue "Growing in Christ While Helping Others."

ALSO AVAILABLE

CELEBRATE RECOVERY 30 ANNIVERSARY

# Celebrate Recovery®

## 365 DAILY DEVOTIONAL

This daily devotional is specially designed to complement the Celebrate Recovery® program. It features 366 brief original readings, each a powerful reminder of God's goodness, grace, and redemption and an inspiration to anyone struggling with old hurts, habits, and hang-ups. The *Celebrate Recovery 365 Daily Devotional* will encourage everyone who is on the road to recovery.

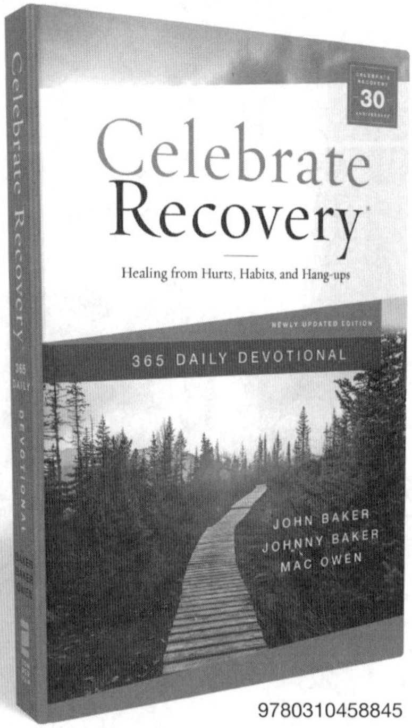


9780310458845

Available now at your favorite bookstore.

ZONDERVAN®